Petworth House

Sussex

THE NATIONAL TRUST

1973

*Petworth House lies 5½ miles east of Midhurst, at
the junction of A272 and A283. The house is open
from April till October on Wednesdays, Thursdays,
Saturdays, Bank Holidays and Connoisseurs' Days
(1st and 3rd Tuesdays in these months), from
2 p.m. until 6 p.m. The deer park is open in daylight
hours all the year round.*

COVER: *Fête in Petworth Park (1835)* by William
Frederick Witherington (1785–1865). (The picture
is No. 2 in the North Gallery.)

ACKNOWLEDGEMENTS

The section on the family history is, apart from
some small additions, that written by Mr. Robin
Fedden for the original National Trust guide book,
and some of the room descriptions are also based
on his text.
For permission to examine the family papers and
accounts I am indebted to the late Lord Egremont,
to Mrs. P. Gill and Mr. D. J. Butler of the West
Sussex Record Office, who were also of great assis-
tance in tracing relevant documents, and to Mr.
John Kenworthy-Browne for helping to revise
the description of the North Gallery. I am in
addition deeply indebted to Miss Dorothy Stroud
for allowing me to make use of her original
researches on Capability Brown for the section on
the park.
Gervase Jackson-Stops.
February, 1973.

*Photographs of the West Front and the Carved
Room by A. F. Kersting*
All other photographs by Jeremy Whitaker

Printed in England at The Curwen Press, London E.13

The Percys, the Seymours and the Wyndhams

The Manor of Petworth was bequeathed by Henry I to his second wife, Queen Adeliza, and she presented it to her brother, Joscelyn, who took the name of Percy when he married Lady Agnes de Percy, heiress of vast possessions in the north. This Lady was the great grand-daughter of the William de Percy (nicknamed Algernon, meaning in Old French 'with the whiskers') who accompanied William of Normandy to England in 1066 and was rewarded with large grants of land in many counties, including those of the Saxon Earl of Northumberland whose daughter he married. So began in 1150 the Percy connection with Petworth. Four generations later, in 1309, Henry Lord Percy obtained a licence to crenellate an existing manor-house, evidence that Petworth had begun to play an important role as one of the Percy seats. The great-grandson of this Lord Percy (and the father of Harry Hotspur) became in 1377 the first of those eleven Earls of Northumberland, rich and powerful nobles, who played such an important role during the three turbulent and factious centuries that followed. They were not fortunate. No fewer than seven of the eleven were killed in battle, executed, murdered or imprisoned; one other, the 6th Earl, died of a broken heart. His misfortunes had included falling in love with Anne Boleyn at the same time as Henry VIII and the execution of his younger brother. Portraits are to be seen at Petworth of the 7th Earl (Oak Staircase Hall, no. 501), the 9th Earl (Oak Staircase Hall, no. 590, and Square Dining room, no. 223), the 10th Earl (Square Dining room, no. 289) and the 11th Earl (Square Dining room, no. 536).

Henry Percy, the 9th Earl, was in many ways the most distinguished of his line; a learned man and a patron of learning he amassed a fine library of books, many of which

3

are still at Petworth. He too was unfortunate in his dealings with higher authority and spent sixteen years in the Tower under suspicion of complicity in the Gunpowder Plot (his cousin was certainly implicated). He was finally released in 1621 on payment of a fine of £11,000, a huge sum in those days which may have thwarted his plans for the rebuilding of Petworth where he spent the remaining eleven years of his life, engaging in those scientific and alchemical experiments which earned him the nickname of the 'Wizard Earl'.

Algernon, the 10th Earl, spent much of his time at Petworth and he and his father must have been responsible for beginning the collection of pictures which is one of its chief glories. He achieved by the uprightness of his character the remarkable feat of earning the respect of both sides in the Civil War and for a time was entrusted by the Parliamentarians with the care of the younger children of Charles I, a task he carried out with the greatest kindness. His son, Joscelyn, survived him by only two years and dying in 1670 at the age of twenty-six left an only daughter, Elizabeth, as heiress of the vast Percy estates.

Sacrificed to her grandmother's ambition, this unhappy child was given in marriage three times in three years, all before her sixteenth birthday. The first, Lord Ogle, died after only a year in 1680; the second, Thomas Thynne, was killed by her lover Königsmarck in the following year; and finally she married in 1682 Charles Seymour, 6th Duke of Somerset. The Duke is chiefly remembered for his obsession with his lineage and his inordinate pride. He is said to have insisted on his children always standing in his presence, and to have cut the inheritance of one of his daughters when he fell asleep and woke to find her seated. The 'Proud Duke' however left behind a splendid monument: it was he who in 1688, when his wife became of age and could dispose of her fortune, set about the rebuilding of Petworth. He also deserves to be remembered for his major benefactions to the University of Cambridge, helping to found the University Press in 1696 and giving huge endowments to Trinity, St Katharine's Hall and other colleges.

When the Duke died in 1748 he was succeeded as 7th Duke by his son Algernon who in the following year was granted by George II, among other honours, the Earldoms of Northumberland and Egremont, but when he died in 1750 he left no son. His estates and titles were thereupon divided, his son-in-law, Sir Hugh Smithson, changing his name to Percy and taking the Earldom of Northumberland and the estates now held by his descendant the present Duke of Northumberland, while Petworth, Cockermouth in Cumberland and other lands, and the Earldom of Egremont went to Charles Wyndham, the son of his sister Catherine.

The Sir William Wyndham whom this lady had married came of an old and distinguished family of consequence in the County of Norfolk who in the sixteenth century had married into a Somersetshire family and settled at the Orchard Wyndham of which a painting (No. 577) can be seen in the Oak Staircase Hall. Sir William like so many of his family from the earliest times, was a Member of Parliament and as a High Tory served under Queen Anne at a very early age as Secretary for War and then Chancellor of the Exchequer. At the accession of George I he was involved in the Jacobite intrigues which culminated in the 1715 Rebellion and was tried and committed to the Tower. His incensed father-in-law, the 'Proud Duke' (who considered the King had broken a pledge to pardon Sir William if he surrendered voluntarily) expressed his resentment with such pungency that he was obliged to give up his Mastership of the Horse and is said to have delivered up his insignia and royal liveries by pitching them into a dustcart and ordering his servants to shoot 'all the rubbish' into the Courtyard of St. James's Palace. Sir William was released the following year and returned to the House of Commons. His Jacobite sympathies cooled but he remained a Tory and as his party did not return to power until after his death he never again held office, but as an active and influential member of the Opposition he was greatly admired and respected by his contemporaries and among many tributes at his death it was Pope who wrote of him 'If I see any man merry within a week after this death, I will affirm him no true patriot'.

Charles Wyndham, second Lord Egremont, though less distinguished than his father, was a capable and likeable man. He played a considerable role in the politics of the eighteenth century and maintained a reputation for honesty at a time when many politicians were corrupt. He succeeded Pitt as Secretary of State for the South in 1761. His official duties involved many banquets and he was heard genially to say, 'Well I have but three turtle dinners to come and if I survive them I shall be immortal'. He did not survive them but died in 1763 leaving a beautiful widow (who married Count Brühl, the Saxon Ambassador) and several children. The eldest child, a boy of twelve, was to rule at Petworth for sixty-five years as the 3rd Earl of Egremont. He was later to use the surname of O'Brien when he inherited the estates of the Earl of Thomond, a family connection established by the marriage of one of the 'Proud Duke's' daughters.

The 3rd Lord Egremont (1751–1837) grew up a remarkable man. Humane, cultured, and distinguished both as patron of the arts and as agriculturist, he introduced a golden age at Petworth.

His hospitality was famous and Burke spoke of him as 'delighting to reign in the dispensation of happiness', while Benjamin Haydon, the history painter, wrote that 'his greatest pleasure was sharing with highest and humblest the luxuries of his vast income. The very animals at Petworth seemed happier than in any other spot on earth.' Though the admired friend of Charles James Fox, Lord Egremont played little part in political life, preferring to receive at Petworth those painters and men of letters whose entertainment has secured him a lasting reputation as a great patron of the arts. Turner was a close friend, and spent much time at Petworth, where he painted several of his most important works. The painters Thomas Phillips and James Northcote, and the sculptor, John Edward Carew, were amongst his other *protégés*. The Earl's other consuming interest was in farming. He was for many years on the Board of Agriculture, where his promotion of new, progressive farming methods (which led to a firm friendship with Arthur Young) was directed always at improving the lot of the small tenant. During the years of deepest agricultural depression he continued to give annual feasts at Petworth for his own tenantry and workers, and one of these is recorded in the picture by Witherington (reproduced on the cover) which hangs in the North Gallery.

In his role as patron particularly, Lord Egremont found support in the taste of the lady who for long bore the courtesy title of Mrs. Wyndham. For some reason Lord Egremont did not marry her until after the birth of six children and on his death the earldom passed to a nephew, and is now extinct. The house and estates passed however to his eldest son, George Wyndham, created Baron Leconfield in 1859. In 1947 the 3rd Lord Leconfield conveyed Petworth, with a large endowment, to the National Trust to be preserved for the nation.

His nephew, John Wyndham, who succeeded to the estates in 1963, was for many years the private secretary and confidant of Harold Macmillan, joining him at the Ministry of Supply in 1940 and following him to the Colonial Office, to Allied Headquarters in Algiers in 1943 and to the Air Ministry in 1945. While his party were out of office, Wyndham joined the Conservative Research Department where he became head of the economic section, and then in 1955 rejoined Mr. Macmillan when the latter was Foreign Secretary and finally Prime Minister. It has been said that 'their friendship and collaboration, that of statesman and private secretary, had no counterpart in modern history'. Wyndham was created Lord Egremont in 1963 and also inherited the Leconfield title on the death of his father in 1967. It was largely through his efforts that the majority of the pictures at Petworth were acquired by the nation in lieu of death duties, a negotiation which was to become an important historical precedent. His eldest son, the present Lord Egremont, still lives in the house, and thus the long Percy-Wyndham connection that has lasted eight centuries continues today.

The House

Between 1688 and 1693 Petworth was almost entirely re-modelled by the Duke of Somerset and it was he who built the magnificent west façade, the original entrance front overlooking the park. Approached from the stables how-ever the back of the house is in surprising contrast with this ducal grandeur, a patchwork of buttresses, brick and stone-work punctuated by windows and doors of every size. This irregularity is a key to the architectural history of the house. To the right of the present visitors' entrance can be seen the traceried east window of the thirteenth-century chapel. This is the only part of the fortified manor-house of the Percys to survive intact above ground, but the cellars under the Carved Room are the undercroft of the medieval Great Hall and those under the other rooms of the west front were built by the 9th Earl in about 1625 as the foundation for his south wing.

In other words the 'Proud Duke's' rebuilding was not as radical as the bland symmetry of the west front suggests. The thickness of many of the walls throughout the house and the lack of symmetrical planning show that he was bound by the site and form of the older house. Entries in the accounts like one 'for taking down three gable heads att ye south end of ye house' in 1691 reveal that even out-side walls of the 9th Earl's wing were retained in the new building. In later years Defoe was to criticize him for not building on an entirely new site further from the town and on higher ground to the north, but like many of his contemporaries the Duke probably hoped to save money and to stress the continuity of family ownership by re-modelling rather than building afresh. By making a long new approach through the park to his show front on the west perhaps he hoped to disguise the fact that the house stood only 50 yards from the town, a site better suited to a medieval fortress than to a country seat.

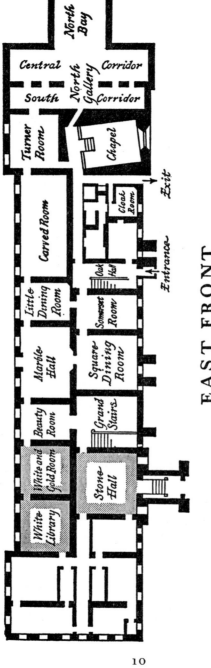

WEST FRONT

EAST FRONT

PETWORTH HOUSE

☐ *Shown on Connoisseurs Day only*

Work began in earnest in 1688 on the coming of age of the Duchess, the Percy heiress whose patrimony had included Petworth, and it must have been mostly completed by 1693 when the Somersets entertained William III here. Almost all the workmen employed are known from the account books and include a number of master-craftsmen of the Board of Works such as Samuel Foulkes, the mason who acted as supervisor at Petworth and who had worked for Wren at Winchester, Edward Dee the bricklayer, John Hunt the glazier and Edward Goudge the plasterer. Unfortunately the architect himself is not known, presumably because he was paid out of the Duke's private purse rather than through any agent or clerk of the works. The mystery is particularly fascinating both because of the very high quality of the design and its unusually French characteristics. The west front is closely related stylistically to Montagu House, Bloomsbury (demolished to make way for the British Museum), and to the remodelled north front of Boughton in Northamptonshire, both built by the Duchess's stepfather, Ralph Montagu. The resemblance to Montagu House must originally have been far closer to judge by a painting of the west front of Petworth in about 1700 which shows a squared dome over the centre three bays, probably the 'Sirculer roofe' for which the slater was paid in 1690. However a disastrous fire in 1714 destroyed part of the centre of the house including the dome, and this much-needed vertical feature in the 320 feet long façade seems not to have been replaced. Two other important changes have since been made to the west front: the ground floor windows have all been lengthened and the roof is now lower-pitched. Originally the sections over the end projections (or 'pavilions') were also completely separated from the main ridge, which gave the house still more of a French look.

Colen Campbell in *Vitruvius Britannicus* ascribed Montagu House to a 'Monsieur Puget', but the architectural work of the sculptor Pierre Puget is so entirely different in style from both Ralph Montagu's houses and from Petworth that he can be discarded as a possibility, whilst no other designer of that name is known. Likewise John Scarborough who was paid for surveying at Petworth in 1690 was almost certainly employed not as a designer but simply as a measurer; he acted several times for Wren in this same capacity. A more likely candidate would be the Comptroller of the Board of Works, William Talman, who worked elsewhere with many of the craftsmen recorded at Petworth and whose courtyard façade at Drayton in Northamptonshire has some features in common with the west front at Petworth.

Recently however another serious contender has been put forward for this group of three houses. This is Daniel Marot, Berain's chief pupil, who fled to Holland after the Revocation of the Edict of Nantes in 1685, soon afterwards became Architect to William of Orange, and spent several short periods in England after William's accession in 1688. Marot is now known to have been employed by Ralph Montagu, a noted Francophile as well as being a close friend of William III, to design a series of painted panels for a room at Montagu House; moreover the arcaded north front of Boughton is very close to an engraving in Marot's *Œuvres*. At Petworth too the ground floor of the north front had a rusticated open arcade before the addition of the 3rd Earl of Egremont's sculpture gallery at this end of the house.

As well as the squared dome which must have compared with Marot's designs for the Hôtel Wassenaar-Obdam at The Hague, almost all the surviving features of the west front at Petworth, such as the brackets carved with masks above the end pavilion windows, the busts in panels below them and the channelled rustication of the centre three bays, can be paralleled in his work, while the Marble Hall, the only important architectural interior to survive the fire of 1714, has affinities with Marot's Trèveszaal in the Binnenhof and his interiors at the palace of Het Loo, both executed for William III in Holland. A further tantalizing scrap of evidence is an entry in the Duke of Somerset's personal account book for Petworth in 1693 recording payment 'to Mr. Maro' of the relatively large sum of £30. Unfortunately there is no clue as to what this payment was for. No positive proof has yet emerged that Marot came to England before his marriage in 1694, yet the building activity at Kensington and Hampton Court (where he is known to have designed the interiors of the Water Gallery and the parterre for Queen Mary) make an earlier visit more than likely. If at the same time he was concerned in the re-building of Petworth this would probably have meant simply drawing up a design which was to be executed (and modified) entirely by native craftsmen. As at Boughton, there are peculiarly English tricks in the masonry and joinery which contrast with the sophisticated, totally French form of the whole building. Possibly the mason-architect William Thornton of York had something to do with this stage of the work for his name appears in a receipt dated 1692, and Beningborough Hall in Yorkshire which he designed and built soon afterwards has a number of Marotesque features that could have been learnt at Petworth. The 'keystones with carved winges' (the Duke's crest) above each window are the work of Selden whose superb woodcarvings can be seen inside the house, and the eagles flanked by busts over the windows of the end pavilions are either by him or by Grinling Gibbons who was paid £173 for 'statues' in 1692. The painting of the house in about 1700 shows elaborate vases and statues along the parapet of this front some of which survive in the gardens.

The exterior of the late seventeenth-century Petworth remained little altered until about 1780 when the 3rd Lord Egremont added the North Gallery to house his father's collection of antique sculpture. This one-storey extension did not spoil the symmetry of the west front but did involve filling in the arches of the open arcade on the ground floor of the north front. The rusticated arches of this arcade seem to have been re-used as the elevation for the new gallery. The Gallery arches originally held windows, but these are now blocked up. With the expansion of his collections to include contemporary English painting and sculpture, Lord Egremont added a further bay to the north in 1824, but Soane's plans of about this date to stucco the west front and add a porch to it were fortunately not carried out. The last major building phase at Petworth was in 1869–72 when Salvin tactfully replanned and rebuilt the south-east part of the house, a restoration apparently made necessary by the porousness of those walls rebuilt after the fire of 1714. The south front is his and so is the new entrance and porte-cochère on the east; previously the principal entry had been into the Marble Hall from the park on the west.

THE INTERIOR

THE OAK STAIRCASE HALL is one of the rooms re-modelled by the 'Proud Duke' between 1688 and 1693. The simple coved ceiling and staircase balustrade are obviously of this date but the great thickness of the walls, seen for instance in the deep window embrasures on the landing, shows that the structure is much earlier in date and part of the old Percy manor-house.

The Hall gives the visitor a foretaste of the magnificent collection of pictures at Petworth. Among the most notable are Lely's *Children of Charles* I (no. 149) and, over the stairs, portraits of the 7th and 9th Earls of Northumberland (nos. 501 and 590). The furniture includes four seventeenth-century Italian chairs, a leather-bound travelling chest, and a long-case clock in burr walnut by Thomas Tompion. In 1687 'Mr. Tompion, for clensing and mending a clocke' at Petworth was paid fifteen shillings; it is more than likely that he also supplied this clock for the Duke of Somerset soon afterwards. The porcelain is mainly Chinese of the seventeenth and early eighteenth centuries, collected by the Duchess who seems to have shared Mary II's passion for oriental porcelain. She must have had a 'china cabinet' in her apartment like the Queen's at Hampton Court loaded with porcelain of every kind from small cups and finger bowls to the huge Kang Hsi mandarin jars which stand here. The bust in the window represents the 3rd Lord Egremont, the patron of Turner and the connoisseur whose collections of paintings and sculpture still enrich Petworth today.

Paintings[1]

Pictures and sculpture are listed in the order in which the visitor will find them as he enters each room, starting at the left.

560 James Seymour (1702–52)
   Racing at Newmarket

405 Dutch School (XVIIth century)
   A bearded Man

163 Manner of Frans Pourbus the Elder (1545–81)
   Bearded Man in black Cap

515 David Teniers (1610–90)
   Landscape with a Cottage
   and

240 *Landscape with a Woman milking*

577 English School (early XVIIIth century)
   Orchard Wyndham in Somerset
   The property came into the Wyndham family in the XVIth century.

[1]Further details of the pictures and classical statuary are to be found respectively in the *Catalogue of the Petworth Collection of Pictures* by C. H. Collins Baker (Medici Society, 1920), and the *Catalogue of the Collection of Greek and Roman Antiquities in the Possession of Lord Leconfield* by Margaret Wyndham (Medici Society, 1915). Numbers refer to these catalogues. For the revision of the sculpture the National Trust is indebted to Professor C. Vermeule's 'Michaelis Notes' in *American Journal of Archaeology*, vols. 59, 60 (1955, 1956), and for permission to use his MS. Notes.

76 David Teniers (1610–90)
    The Archduke Leopold's Gallery
    The Archduke Leopold-William, Governor of the Netherlands
    from 1646–56, was a noted collector. Teniers, who was keeper
    of the collection, painted the scene on several occasions.

149 Sir Peter Lely (1618–80)
    The Youngest Children of Charles I in 1647
    James, Duke of York (1633–1701); Elizabeth (1635–50);
    Henry, Duke of Gloucester (1639–60).

101 Artist Unknown
    Ralph, 1st Baron Hopton (1598–1652)
    A noted Royalist general.

361 Studio of Sir Peter Lely (1618–80)
    An unknown Girl

98 Manner of Sir Anthony Van Dyck (1599–1641)
    *Lodovick Stuart, 2nd Duke of Lennox and Duke of
    Richmond (1574–1624)*
    Steward of the Household to James I.

590 (?) Dutch School (1602)
    Henry Percy, 9th Earl of Northumberland (1564–1632)
    The 'Wizard Earl'.

501 George Gower (1540–96)
    Thomas Percy, 7th Earl of Northumberland (1528–72)
    A prominent Catholic; beheaded for his support of Mary
    Queen of Scots.

517 Frans Snyders (1579–1657)
    Concert of Birds

591 Benjamin West (1738–1820)
    The Nativity
    Cartoon for window in St. George's Chapel, Windsor.

Sculpture

113 *Bust of the 3rd Earl of Egremont (1826)*
    By William Behnes (d. 1864)

THE SOMERSET ROOM and the room which follows it
were created early in the nineteenth century out of what was
the largest room in the house according to Laguerre's ground
plan on the Great Staircase, probably the Duke of Somerset's

The West Front

Detail of Laguerre's painting on the Grand Staircase showing the West Front as originally built.

Photograph: Country Life

dining room. The chimneypiece and colza-oil chandelier must date from the time of the alteration, towards the end of the 3rd Lord Egremont's life. The room has now been arranged as a picture gallery to show mainly paintings of the seventeenth-century Dutch School, including important works by Hobbema and Cuyp (nos. 114 and 207). Near the window hangs the magnificent *Landscape with Jacob and Laban* by Claude (no. 329), and a showcase contains eight small pictures by Elsheimer.

Between the windows are a splendid mid-eighteenth-century rococo pier-glass and console table. Altogether there are eight different glasses of this date in the house, all of superb quality and near in style to the designs of Thomas Johnson. They were probably supplied, with pier tables, by a leading London maker between 1755 and 1758 when the 2nd Earl of Egremont is known to have made alterations to the house. The pair of gilt console tables on the wall opposite the chimneypiece are also part of this set. The bureaux on the other side of the room are in the manner of A. C. Boulle; that nearer the window is of the Louis XIV period and its top has a *singerie* design very close to those of Berain. The sofa and fauteuils are also French, of the Louis XVI period. The porcelain on the giltwood console tables is part of a late Sèvres service. The elaborately decorated porcelain on the chimneypiece and on the French inlaid furniture is Worcester.

Paintings

385 Sir Ralph Cole (1625?–1704)
Thomas Wyndham
Brother of Sir William Wyndham, 1st Bart.

203 Adam van der Meulen (1632–90)
Louis XIV Stag Hunting at Fontainebleau

207 Attributed to Aelbert Cuyp (1620–91)
View of a River Town

167 Sir Anthony Van Dyck (1599–1641)
A Genoese Lady

388 Lucas van Uden (1595–1672)
A Procession passing through a Wood
The figure on the prancing horse is probably Gaston d'Orléans
(1608–60), who was granted asylum by the Spanish at Brussels
in the early 1630s.

48 Jacob van Ruisdael (1628/9–82)
Waterfall

15 Meindert Hobbema (1638–1709)
Landscape with a Coppice

451 Philips de Koninck (1619–88/9)
Woman with a Rosebud

312 Attributed to Cornelis Saftleven (1607–81)
An Allegory of the Martyrdom of Charles I
The scene is probably intended to represent the disasters
succeeding the execution of the king. A wolf (representing
Cromwell or the Republic?) savours a portrayal of the incident,
while beside it lie the works of the Reformers and the overthrown
scales of justice. Lawlessness and brutality result; from the
mouth of Hell issue forth famine, ignorance and attendant horrors
and vices; and retribution follows in the burning of London
(Painted after 1666).

205 Adam van der Meulen (1632–90)
Louis XIV at Maestricht

114 Aelbert Cuyp (1620–91)
Landscape near Nymwegen

272–9 Adam Elsheimer (*c.* 1578–1610)
Eight Religious Subjects

85 Adam van der Meulen (1632–90)
Bandits holding up Travellers

329 Claude Gelée, called Claude Lorrain (1600–82)
Jacob with Laban and his Daughters

514 Cornelis Dusart (1660–1704)
A Country Inn

73 David Teniers (1610–90)
Sand Cliff and Figures

99 Follower of Sir Anthony Van Dyck (1599–1641)
Lady Mary Villiers, Duchess of Richmond (d. 1685)
Daughter of 1st Duke of Buckingham.

379 David Teniers (1610–90)
A Peasant filling his Pipe

THE SQUARE DINING ROOM, despite its seventeenth-century appearance, was formed and decorated early in the nineteenth century by the 3rd Earl. The curtain boxes carved with fruit, flowers and dead game in the style of Grinling Gibbons are by Jonathan Ritson, a gifted carver from Cumberland employed by Lord Egremont for many years to repair and reinstate the work of Gibbons and Selden elsewhere in the house. The chimneypiece of yellow Siena and white marble with a central plaque of Mercury is much earlier however and in the style of Sir Henry Cheere. It must be contemporary with the three gilt rococo glasses in this room, again of about 1755. The pier-glasses have wings carved on the cross-bars between the two panes, an allusion to the family crest which show that they were made especially for the house. The pair of white painted Kent sideboards flanking the chimneypiece are probably earlier still, about 1725, though the other sideboards around the room were made later to match.

The family silver displayed is mainly by Paul Storr, who between 1807 and 1814 made for Lord Egremont the candelabra (both silver and gold), and the twelve wine coolers. The silver-gilt cups also date from the early nineteenth century. The large 'Monteith' bowl in the middle of the dining-table (1710) is by J. Wisdom. The 'Monteith' bowls on the side-tables bear the date marks for 1693 and 1767.

The splendid Van Dycks in this room were acquired by the Percys and must have hung originally in the old house: the two portraits of Sir Robert and Lady Shirley (nos. 96 and 97) are early, and show the artist working on an unusually exotic theme. The *Thomas Wentworth, Earl of Strafford* (no. 311) is among the artist's most sensitive character studies. No. 223, a posthumous picture, probably after an earlier model, represents the 'Wizard Earl' himself as he appeared in his later years. Many of the pictures have kept their original seventeenth-century frames; Verelst's portrait of Prince Rupert (no. 342) has an especially noteworthy one carved with putti and palm fronds.

Paintings

525 Sir Peter Lely (1618–80)
Lady Anne Percy, Countess of Chesterfield (1633–54)
Daughter of 10th Earl of Northumberland.

593 English School
Sir Charles Percy (d. 1628)
Fourth son of 8th Earl of Northumberland

96 Sir Anthony Van Dyck (1599–1641)
Sir Robert Shirley (1581?–1628)
He was for many years employed as diplomatic agent by the Shah of Persia.

522 School of Sir Anthony Van Dyck (1599–1641)
An unknown Man

97 Sir Anthony Van Dyck (1599–1641)
Elizabeth, or Teresia, Lady Shirley
Circassian wife of Sir Robert Shirley.

524 Sir Peter Lely (1618–80)
Lady Elizabeth Percy, Countess of Essex (1636–1718)
Daughter of 10th Earl of Northumberland.

461 Sir Peter Lely (1618–80)
   Elizabeth Alington, Lady Seymour of Trowbridge (c. *1632–91*)
   Mother of the 5th and 6th Dukes of Somerset.

536 (?) Sir Peter Lely (1618–80)
   Joscelyn Percy, 11th Earl of Northumberland (*1644–70*)

311 Sir Anthony Van Dyck (1599–1641)
   Thomas Wentworth, 1st Earl of Strafford (*1593–1641*)

342 Simon Verelst (1643–c. 1695)
   Prince Rupert (*1619–82*)

670 Jacques d'Artois (1613–86)
   Landscape with Hunting Party

295 Sir Anthony Van Dyck (1599–1641)
   Catherine Bruce, Countess of Dysart (*d. after 1651*)

223 Sir Anthony Van Dyck (1599–1641)
   Henry Percy, 9th Earl of Northumberland (*1564–1632*)
   The 'Wizard Earl'.

159 Studio of Sir Peter Lely (1618–80)
   Sir William Wyndham, 1st Bart. (*1632–83*)

285 Studio of Sir Anthony Van Dyck (1599–1641)
   Sir Charles Percy (*d. 1628*)
   Fourth son of 8th Earl of Northumberland.

220 Sir Anthony Van Dyck (1599–1641)
   Lady Dorothy Percy, Countess of Leicester (*1598–1659*)
   Daughter of 9th Earl of Northumberland.

289 Sir Anthony Van Dyck (1599–1641)
   Algernon Percy, 10th Earl of Northumberland (*1602–68*),
   Lady Anne Cecil, his first wife, and their daughter

521 Studio of Sir Peter Lely (1618–80)
   Lady Elizabeth Wriothesley, Viscountess Campden (*d. 1680*)
   Sister of wife of 11th Earl of Northumberland.

288 Studio of Sir Anthony Van Dyck (1599–1641)
   Lady Ann Cavendish, Lady Rich (*1612–38*)

300 Sir Anthony Van Dyck (1599–1641)
   Mountjoy Blount, Earl of Newport (*d. 1666*), *George, Lord
   Goring* (*1608–57*), *and a Page*
   Prominent royalist commanders.

297 Sir Anthony Van Dyck (1599–1641)
   Henry, Baron Percy of Alnwick (*d. 1659*)
   Second son of 9th Earl of Northumberland.

THE MARBLE HALL dates almost entirely from the time of the Duke of Somerset, whose supporters, the bull and the unicorn, appear over the chimneypieces. It is the only important seventeenth-century architectural interior in the house to survive both the fire of 1714 and the early nineteenth-century alterations of the 3rd Earl. The decoration is full of baroque French and Dutch features found only rarely in English houses of this date, and these strengthen the possibility that Daniel Marot, a Huguenot émigré to Holland could have made the designs for the re-modelling of Petworth in 1688—the year that his master William III ascended the English throne. The mouldings, carved in great depth by Selden, are over life-size and their scale increases towards the ceiling so that the frieze is of huge acanthus brackets supported by an egg and tongue moulding of heroic proportions. Both this frieze and the two overmantels, with semi-circular-topped frames cutting into bold segmental pediments, appear in the so called Trèveszaal, or audience chamber of the States-General, which Marot added to the Binnenhof at The Hague in 1696–98. Marot's designs for the dining room at De Voorst, the Earl of Albemarle's hunting lodge near Zutphen, are also reminiscent of the Marble Hall. They too have a bold bracketed frieze, but also share the square overdoor frames with flamboyant acanthus surrounds, and the very Dutch feature of a marble skirting to the walls at Petworth. The illusionism of the deeply splayed window recesses and niche for the door to the dining room are particularly baroque; indeed the room as a whole is perhaps the nearest approach in this country to the full-blown Louis XIV style.

The accounts for the 'Hall of State', as it was originally described, are very full as far as the names of craftsmen are concerned. In 1692 John Selden was paid £50 for wood-carving in this room alone, Nicholas Mitchell for the 'dove-coloured' bolection chimneypieces, Thomas Larkin for wainscoting, Edward Goudge for plasterwork, George Tourner for painting, 'Mr. Stroud' for the marble paving and John Madgwick for 'beateing down pte of the wall in the hall of State for the neeces'. The chased lock-plates, here as in several other rooms, bear the Duke of Somerset's arms and were probably made at the same time by the locksmith, John Draper. By the spring of the following year when William III came to Petworth this room must have looked very much as it does today.

Royalty again came to the Marble Hall when Lord Egremont received the Allied Sovereigns here in 1814, an event recorded in Phillips's picture in the North Gallery. Its appearance a generation later can be seen in the water-colour drawing by Mrs. Percy Wyndham which shows that it was then used as a breakfast room. The set of white-painted rococo stools in this picture are still in the same positions as in the picture, and were probably made for the room in the 1750s and the organ, no longer in working order, was built by John England in 1784. The statuary and funerary urns are Roman, dating from the first to the third centuries A.D.

Paintings

189 Sir Joshua Reynolds (1723–92)
     2nd Earl of Guilford (1739–92)
     Lord North, Prime Minister, 1770–82.

188 Manner of Titian (*c.* 1487–1576)
     A Cardinal

154 Sir Joshua Reynolds (1723–92)
     Col. Alexander Dow (d. 1779)

168 Sir Joshua Reynolds (1723–92)
     James Macpherson, M.P. (1736–96)

123 J. A. van Ravesteyn (*c.* 1572–1657)
     David de Ruyter (c. 1580–1663)
     Dutch lawyer.

187 Sir Joshua Reynolds (1723–92)
     An Officer

23

Sculpture

THE BEAUTY ROOM is so called after the series of portraits by Sir Godfrey Kneller and Michael Dahl, the Swedish painter, which hang here above the panelling. They represent ladies of the Court of Queen Anne, amongst whom the Duchess of Somerset was a familiar figure. Over the chimneypiece is the Queen herself (no. 208) and, opposite, the Duchess of Marlborough (no. 197). Other pictures include a portrait of a man in a black plumed hat by Titian (no. 298), a *Peasant Family* by Louis Le Nain (no. 48) and a small landscape by Salomon van Ruysdael (no. 441).

The plain coved ceiling and the absence of an elaborate frieze in this room probably mean that it was gutted in the fire of 1714 and reformed soon afterwards. Above the large doorway to the staircase is an oblong carved panel by Selden with two putti emerging from a rich acanthus background and supporting the Duke and Duchess of Somerset's monogram encircled by the Garter; it may have formed part of the original overmantel in the Little Dining Room removed later in the eighteenth century for it matches the carving of the frieze in that room. The seventeenth-century marble bolection chimneypiece and the landscape

South West Pavilion

glass above it have recently been reinstated in place of a nineteenth-century arrangement and at the same time the room has been redecorated using a pale terra-cotta colour scheme.

On the central table stands the famous 'Leconfield Aphrodite', the outstanding piece of ancient sculpture in the house. Scholars agree that it is certainly by the same hand as the Hermes at Olympia attributed to Praxiteles, and dates from the fourth century B.C. The hall chairs are part of a large set painted with the Percy crest and an earl's coronet. They were probably made for the 9th Earl and as such are rare examples of early Stuart painted furniture, much influenced by Italian models. Between the windows is a very fine rococo pier table of the mid-eighteenth century, and there are also two black lacquer chests one on an early eighteenth-century stand.

Looking back from the Beauty Room through the door to the Marble Hall the immense *enfilade* of the rooms on the west front becomes apparent. From the White Library in the family's private apartments one can see through seven great doors set on a dead straight line, a distance of about 300 feet, to a colossal third-century Roman bust in the North Gallery.

Paintings

195 Michael Dahl (*c.* 1659–1743)
Jane Temple, Countess of Portland (1672–1751)

196 Michael Dahl (*c.* 1659–1743)
Lady Mary Somerset, Duchess of Ormonde (1665–1733)

197 Sir Godfrey Kneller (1646–1723)
Sarah Jennings, Duchess of Marlborough (1660–1744)

201 Michael Dahl (*c.* 1659–1743)
Rachel Russell, Duchess of Devonshire (1674–1725)

202 Michael Dahl (*c.* 1659–1743)
Lady Ann Capel, Countess of Carlisle (1674–1752)
Grand-daughter of 11th Earl of Northumberland.

THE GRAND STAIRCASE is decorated with murals by Louis Laguerre, who was employed by the Duke of Somerset after the fire of 1714 had destroyed the old staircase. The lower part is decorated with scenes from the story of Prometheus (perhaps an allusion to the fire), the landing with the Muses, and the ceiling with a scene showing the Assembly of the Gods; while on the south wall the Duchess of Somerset rides in a triumphal chariot attended by her children and her very life-like spaniel. The staircase at Petworth was considered by Vertue to be one of Laguerre's best works; a sketch for it by the artist is now at the British Museum.

The balustrade is nineteenth century and the design for it seems to have come from the office of Sir Charles Barry for drawings for it survive in the Barry collection at the R.I.B.A. The carpet at the foot of the stairs is a rare Exeter imitation of Savonnerie made in 1758, and the furniture includes two very fine seventeenth-century Japanese lacquer cabinets on carved ebonised stands. These may have been supplied by Gerrit Jensen whose bills survive for a large quantity of tables, mirrors and stands in 1690, including a set with silver mounts which has since disappeared.

Sculpture

66 *Portrait Bust of a late Severan Lady*
Perhaps Julia Paula, wife of Elagabalus (A.D. 218–22)
Bust, Trajanic or Hadrianic, does not belong.

54 *Seilenos Liknophoros*
Roman, 2nd century A.D.

32 *Bust of a Bacchante*
Head from statue group (?), set on a modern bust.

106 *The Rt. Hon. William Huskisson, M.P.* (1770–1830)
By Samuel Joseph (d. 1850)

71 *Youth Crowned with a Laurel Wreath*
Julio-Claudian period (Bust restored).

(From the Grand Staircase the visitor returns through the Beauty Room and the Marble Hall.)

THE LITTLE DINING ROOM (formerly the Van Dyck Room) contains a selection of the earlier pictures in the Petworth collection: a version of the Adoration of the Magi attributed to Bosch (no. 63), two panels by Rogier van der Weyden (no. 122 a & b: a copy of the missing fragment of the Angel of the Annunciation is in Berlin), and several small sixteenth-century portraits of the German, Flemish and French Schools.

This room is basically as it was in the Duke of Somerset's time except that Laguerre's ground plan of about 1715 shows it with a corner chimneypiece. The present white marble chimneypiece is mid-eighteenth century in date. The extraordinarily elaborate carved frieze and cornice with the Duke's monogram repeated four times in a luxuriant background of acanthus and flowers can safely be attributed to John Selden. This carver of genius is described by Walpole in his *Anecdotes of Painting* as Gibbons's 'disciple and assistant' but it seems more probable that, like Samuel Watson at Chatsworth, he was a local craftsman who worked independently and exclusively at Petworth, producing anything from table frames to stone gate-piers. The boldness of the mouldings in this room are perhaps equalled only by those at Beningborough in Yorkshire, a house built to designs by a carpenter and joiner, William Thornton of York in the following decade. Thornton's name appears once ambiguously in the Petworth accounts for 1692 but it is tempting to associate him in some way with Selden, possibly even as his apprentice.

Between the windows is another rococo gilt pier-glass of which there are so many fine examples in the house. This one is particularly chinoiserie in style with a hissing ho-ho bird perched on the top cresting. The three white-painted side tables with marble tops are early eighteenth century and the gilt table in the centre on unusual sphinx supports is French probably of about the same period. The tureens on the centre table are Chelsea, and the rest of the porcelain here is Meissen.

Paintings

327 (?) North Italian (XVIth century)
Unknown lady

63 Attributed to Hieronymus Bosch (*c.* 1450–1516)
Adoration of the Kings

122A and 122B Rogier van der Weyden (1399–1464)
The Virgin Annunciate; St. James with a Donor (*fragments*)

406 Venetian School (XVIth century)
Man with a Letter

174 German School (XVIth century)
Bearded Man with blue Flower

306 Simon de Vlieger (1601–53)
Seascape

79 Jean François Millet (1642–79)
Italian Scene

318 Juan Pantoja de la Cruz (1553–1608)
Clara Isabella Eugenia, Archduchess of Austria (1566–1633)

438 Ludolf Bakhuysen (1631–1708)
Seascape

18 Sebastien Bourdon (1616–71)
The Selling of Joseph

171 German School (XVIth century)
Man with a hooded Hawk

61 Unknown (Early XVIIth century)
1st Lord Hopton

322 Joos van Cleef (*c.* 1485–1540)
Man with an Emerald Ring

181 After Hans Holbein (1497–1543)
Thomas Cromwell, Earl of Essex (c. *1485–1540*)

440 Contemporary of Hans Eworth (op. *c.* 1540–73)
(?) *Chideok Tichborne*

47 Jan Matsys (op. *c.* 1510–75)
Card Players, or The Prodigal Son

175 Joos van Cleef (*c.* 1485–1540)
Man with a Letter

123 After Hans Memling (1430/5–94)
Man in a black Cap

Sculpture

THE CARVED ROOM assumed its present shape only late in the eighteenth century. It was probably the 3rd Earl again who was responsible for throwing two rooms into one and forming this gallery, at the same time as he built an extension on the north of the house for his sculpture collection. Laguerre's ground plan distinctly shows two rooms here in 1715 and Dallaway in his *History of Western Sussex* of 1832 admits that this was originally so. This would explain the awkward fenestration of the room with a wider gap between door and window at the north than at the south. The carving here is therefore an assembly of pieces from different parts of the house and from three separate hands. It includes not only Grinling Gibbons's superlative pair of double picture frames either side of the chimneypiece but also magnificent naturalistic work, also in limewood, by John Selden and his early nineteenth-century successor at Petworth, Jonathan Ritson, whom the 3rd Earl brought from Cumberland.

Gibbons's work all on the long east wall is instantly recognizable by its inimitably bold technique, larger scale and more confident composition than the rest. The great set piece on the left surmounting Riley and Closterman's portraits of the 'Proud Duke' and his wife has an immense pair of wings, the Duke's crest, at its centre from which hang his star of the Garter and his 'George'; all around both pictures cascade flowers and fruit and above them ducal coronets are held aloft by palms so thinly cut they seem to defy the medium. Lower down between the two frames hang a pair of classical vases, carved almost in the round, an allusion perhaps to the Duke's patronage of the arts; Horace Walpole considered them in 'the purest taste, and worthy of the Grecian age of Cameos'. On the other side of the chimneypiece the Duke's grandparents, Lord and Lady Seymour of Trowbridge, are given a hardly less sumptuous setting: putti with trumpets sounding their praises, sheafs of musical instruments, songbirds and baskets of flowers. The two pendants in the corners are also by Gibbons: originally they and the double frames must have been disposed around the four walls of a smaller square room, possibly the State Bedchamber or the ante room to it, where their scale would have been still more telling. Despite this they constitute perhaps the greatest of Gibbons's surviving masterpieces, in Walpole's words again 'the most superb monument of his skill'. His bills do not appear in the general building accounts but an entry in the Duke of Somerset's personal receipt book for December 1692 mentions 'a Bill paid to Mr. Gibbons for carveing £150'. In the previous year, 1691, Gibbons had been employed on the Library at Trinity College, Cambridge and it may well be that the Duke, who was Chancellor of the University at that time and a considerable benefactor of Trinity, first encountered him there.

Most of the rest of the carving around the walls is by John Selden, whose talent was hardly less than Gibbons's own, and whose highly baroque style almost amounting to *trompe-l'œil* owes much to the master. The surround to the portrait of Henry VIII over the chimneypiece on the east wall is fairly certainly identifiable with the 'large chimneypiece for the dining roome carved with ffowles ffishes and flowers' for which Selden was paid in the accounts for 1689–90 and its pendants of lobsters, crabs, sole and partridges are amazingly skilled. The overdoors must also be by him and those at the north end of the room with draperies at the sides may be those in the accounts 'carved with fouldings and flowers'. High up between the central windows too is an elaborate trophy with the Duke's arms and coronet, possibly one of 'two large pannells designed for the Hall of State but now sett by' in Selden's bills for 1696. Selden was reported by Vertue to have lost his life in the fire of 1714 while trying to save his carvings, but the parish register at Petworth shows that he lived for a full year after the fire, dying in January 1715.

Ritson's work for the 3rd Earl must have been to reinstate all these carvings of Gibbons and Selden in their new setting, restore them where necessary, and execute more in a vaguely seventeenth-century style to fill the gaps between. A watercolour drawing of the room by Mrs Percy Wyndham in about 1860 shows almost every inch of the walls and ceiling crowded with carved decoration. Most of this was removed a few years later though Ritson's decorations in the cove remain and the cornice is probably also his. Lord Egremont thought highly enough of his talents to have portraits of him and Gibbons painted by George Clint and hung together at the entrance to the room.

The furniture includes a pair of scaled walnut pedestals probably made about 1700 to support the mandarin jars bought by the Duchess of Somerset; a set of carved walnut armchairs with tapestry covers of about 1755 and a pair of contemporary gilt rococo torchères; two George III gilt side tables with porphyry tops; a Louis XIV side table with the cross of Lorraine in the carved decoration of the legs; and an elaborate Boulle commode originally at Hamilton Palace. The gilt firescreen contains a piece of needlework by her late Majesty Queen Mary who presented it to

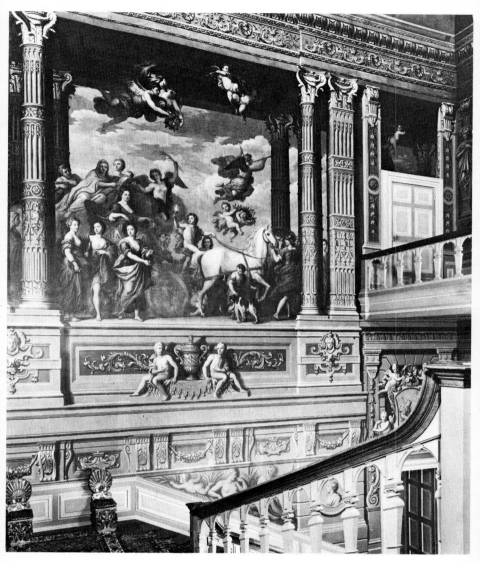

The Grand Staircase

Petworth. The bronze relief of Andromeda is sixteenth-century Flemish, and the other bronzes date from the eighteenth or early nineteenth century. The firebacks bear the crest and initials of the 9th Earl of Northumberland and are survivors from the old Percy house.

Paintings

147B George Clint (1770–1854)
Grinling Gibbons (1648–1721)

147C George Clint (1770–1854)
Jonathan Ritson (c. 1780–1846)
(Nos. 147B and C are to the left of the door.)

147 Sir Peter Lely (1618–80)
Lady Mary Cecil, Lady Sandys

146 Charles Jervas (c. 1675–1739), after Van Dyck
Queen Henrietta Maria (1609–69) and Jeffery Hudson, her Dwarf (1619–82)

145 Sir Peter Lely (1618–80)
Known as Lady Elizabeth Murray, Duchess of Lauderdale (c. 1630–98)

12 Sir Joshua Reynolds (1723–92)
George, 1st Earl Macartney (1737–1806)

139 Attributed to William Larkin (op. 1610–20)
Frances Prinne, Lady Seymour of Trowbridge (d. 1626)

141 Manner of William Larkin (op. 1610–20)
Francis, 1st Baron Seymour of Trowbridge (1590?–1664)

90 Sir Joshua Reynolds (1723–92)
Kitty Fisher (c. 1741–67)
A famous eighteenth-century courtesan.

135 School of Holbein (1497–1543)
Henry VIII (1491–1547)

666 Sir Joshua Reynolds (1723–92)
A Naval Officer

129 J. B. Closterman (c. 1660–1711)
Charles Seymour, 6th Duke of Somerset (1662–1748) with Negro Page

33

127 (?) John Riley (1646–91) and J. B. Closterman (*c.* 1660–1711)
Elizabeth Percy, Duchess of Somerset (1667?–1722) and her
son Algernon Seymour, 7th Duke of Somerset (1684–1750)
The 7th Duke served with Marlborough, achieved the rank of
general, and became Governor of Minorca.

112 Sir Joshua Reynolds (1723–92)
Portrait of a Girl ('Reflection')

126 Sir Peter Lely (1618–80)
Known as Marchioness of Annandale

124 After Sir Anthony Van Dyck (1599–1641)
Charles I on Horseback (1600–49)

125 Sir Peter Lely (1618–80)
Lady Elizabeth Wriothesley, Countess of Northumberland
(1646–90)
Wife of 11th Earl of Northumberland.

THE TURNER ROOM is devoted entirely to the works
of J. M. W. Turner (1775–1851) who was a constant visitor
to Petworth in the 1830s through the friendship and
patronage of the 3rd Earl of Egremont. Turner had his
own studio in the house, the old library above the chapel
with its strong north-east light, and became deeply attached
to his octogenarian mentor, heading the group of artists at
Egremont's funeral in 1837. Many stories are told of him
fishing and making toy boats for children on the lake; and
there is no doubt that Petworth represented not only one
of the happiest periods of his life but also one of his most
unfailing sources of inspiration. The watercolour sketches
of interiors at Petworth, contained in a famous sketchbook
now at the British Museum, are revolutionary in their
effects of light and colour, no less than the two glowing oils
of sunset over the park which hang in this room (nos. 132
and 142). A work of twenty years earlier (no. 653) represents Cockermouth Castle, Lord Egremont's seat in Cumberland.

The panelling, the frieze, cornice and cove, and the
bolection chimneypiece, with acanthus in bold relief all

date from between 1688 and 1693, the period of the 'Proud Duke's' rebuilding. Presumably the carving is again by Selden though the accounts do not make this clear. Between the windows is yet another rococo pier-glass, perhaps the most spectacular in the house with three ho-ho birds holding garlands of flowers in their beaks. The carved walnut armchairs and settee are a continuation of the suite in the Carved Room dating also from about 1755 and the Carlton House desk is of about 1810. On the early Victorian rosewood centre table is a modern bronze of a naiad riding a dolphin.

Paintings

672 *Sea Piece, probably Margate (?1808)*

142 *The Lake, Petworth: Sunset, a Stag Drinking (1830–31)*

  8 *Tabley House and Lake* (c. *1808*)

132 *The Lake, Petworth: Sunset, fighting Bucks* (c. *1830–31*)

658 *Teignmouth Harbour (1812)*

140 *Brighton from the Sea (1830–31)*

  5 *The Thames at Weybridge* (c. *1808*)

108 *The Thames at Eton (?1808)*

665 *The Confluence of the Thames and Medway* (c. *1808*)

  4 *The Thames at Windsor* (c. *1805*)

653 *Cockermouth Castle (1810)*

649 *Windsor Castle (1809)*

130 *Chichester Canal* (c. *1830–31*)

Sculpture

Satyr & Maenad
Roman.
The Sleeping Venus
Italian, 17th or 18th century.
George O'Brien, 3rd Earl of Egremont (1751–1837)
By John Edward Carew (1785–1868)

THE NORTH GALLERY was the 3rd Lord Egremont's creation. It houses paintings and sculpture, notably contemporary works which he collected, but also antique sculptures acquired earlier by the 2nd Earl. Despite alterations and rearrangements it was rightly described by the late Mr. Hussey as 'the finest surviving expression of early nineteenth-century taste', and is one of the few important galleries formed by connoisseurs of that period to have survived intact.

The Gallery was built in two phases: when the 3rd Lord Egremont was unpacking his father's marbles about 1780, he converted an open arcade on the ground floor of the seventeenth-century north front into what is now the south corridor, and added the central section of the Gallery parallel to and beyond it; then about 1824, to accommodate his new pieces of contemporary sculpture he threw out the spacious North Bay. At one time there were windows in the walls; and the North Bay was lit by semi-circular lunettes, which show in a watercolour by Turner in the British Museum. The skylights too were high square wells, as shown in the watercolour by Mrs. Percy Wyndham on the table at the west end of the central corridor; the present ones are replacements of this century. Also at some later date the original dark Pompeian red of the walls was abandoned in favour of pale green, but a recent restoration has returned to the terra-cotta colour so favoured for the display of paintings and sculpture at the turn of the eighteenth and nineteenth centuries.

Among the artists represented in the Gallery are Gainsborough, Reynolds, Wilson, Zoffany, Romney and Fuseli, as well as painters such as Northcote, Callcott, Allston and Loutherbourg who were famous in their day, and Thomas Phillips who was almost official portrait painter to Lord Egremont, and painted him on many occasions (see nos. 562, 57, 309 and 695). William Blake is represented by three watercolours including *The Last Judgement* (no. 454) executed for the Countess of Egremont in 1808. Turner's portrait of *Jessica* also hangs here, together with four more of his landscapes.

The sculpture collection is in two parts: ancient and modern. The ancient marbles here, and those at Newby and Holkham, are the only private eighteenth-century gallery collections remaining in this country, and belong to the period aptly described by Michaelis as 'the golden age of classic dilettantism'. They were collected chiefly about 1750–60 by the 2nd Earl, who employed as agent the younger Matthew Brettingham, then resident in Rome. Brettingham had also acted in this capacity for Thomas Coke of Holkham: but the Petworth collection is the more extensive, and was among the largest in England. The provenance of many of the pieces is unknown, but one at least was excavated by Gavin Hamilton in Rome (no. 6), and the Italian dealer-restorer Cavaceppi obtained others from the Albani (no. 41) and Barberini (nos. 15 & 19) families. *The Pan and Daphnis* (no. 66) was bought in 1801 from Roehampton House. Nearly all the pieces have been restored, some of them in Rome, but others were 'completed' for the 3rd Earl in London by John Edward Carew.

The quality is not uniformly high, but some good and important works reached the collection. The outstanding ancient sculpture is the *Head of Aphrodite*, attributed to Praxiteles (4th Century B.C.) now shown in the Beauty Room. Among the remainder there are some good copies of Hellenic works, including the *Head of an Athlete* (no. 24), the bronze original perhaps by Kresilas (5th Century B.C.); an *Athlete* (9), after an original probably by Polycleitus (5th Century B.C.); *Satyr Pouring Wine* (6) after Praxiteles, but the head and arms eighteenth-century restorations carried out for Gavin Hamilton; Amazon (18), after a 5th Century B.C. original. The *'Apollo Egremont'* (5), playing a lyre, is probably Roman, 2nd Century A.D. The majority of the busts are Roman portraits. There are also two Greek marble reliefs, one of a hero in the style of the Parthenon frieze about the 5th Century B.C., the other from the Acropolis, inscribed with decrees relating to a Panathenaic festival in 94 B.C.

The modern sculpture can be compared with the contemporary galleries at Woburn and Chatsworth; but whereas in the other two Italian figures are predominant, Lord Egremont from about 1814 patronized exclusively English sculptors. The outstanding piece is the great *St. Michael and Satan* by Flaxman in the North Bay, being one of the last works this sculptor completed before his death. There is also his *Pastoral Apollo,* 1824. Sir Richard Westmacott has a *Nymph and Cupid* (North Bay) and a relief of the *Dream of Horace* (Central Corridor) in a mixed style, partly ideal, partly natural. Rossi's group *Celadon and Amelia* shows the storm scene from Thomson's *Seasons.* The other nineteenth-century sculptor represented here, John Edward Carew, was an Irishman whom Lord Egremont employed exclusively from 1822. His *Adonis* and *Arethusa* are in the gallery.

The large terrestrial globe was made by Emery Molyneux in 1592. Molyneux was the first maker of globes in England, and this specimen is believed to be the oldest surviving example of his handiwork. Tradition has it that the globe was given to the 'Wizard Earl' by Sir Walter Raleigh when they were both prisoners in the Tower. There is much to support this supposition. The small globe (presented by the 5th Lord Leconfield) was made by Nathaniel Hill about 1750, and shows the track of Anson's voyage round the world, 1740–44.

In the passage leading out of the North Gallery is a piece of needlework traditionally ascribed to Lady Jane Grey.

Sculpture
The first number in each case is for identification purposes and is reconcilable with the gilt numbered tablet.

1 *Statue of an Athlete* (*The Petworth Oil-Pourer*) (9)
Copy of bronze attributed to the circle of Polykleitos.

2 *Terminal bust of Apollo* (20)
Roman adaptation of Greek 4th century B.C. modification of 5th century type.

3 *Double Terminal head: Dionysos and Ariadne (or Maenad)* (22)
Roman 2nd century A.D. after archaic Greek original.

4 *Term of the Bearded Dionysos* (21)
Major portions ancient, in the manner of the 5th century B.C.

5 *Portrait Head of a Roman* (38)
c. A.D. 235–50.

6 *Bust of an Antonine Prince* (63)

7 *The Emperor Clodius Albinus (d. A.D. 197)* (39)
(Alien bust of same period.)

8 *Bust of an Antonine Prince* (42)

9 *Portrait Bust of a Roman Matron* (61)
Trajanic Period (A.D. 98–117.)

10 *Bust of a Man* (34)
Possibly a Greek portrait of the Hadrianic period.

11 *Portrait Bust of a Roman Matron* (62)
Antonine (?) head on bust of Trajanic period.

12 *Head of the Elder Faustina* (70)
Wife of the Emperor Antoninus Pius (A.D. 138–161); probably a Renaissance portrait done from a coin.

13 *Portrait Bust of a Man* (26)
Roman, mid-3rd century A.D.

14 *Head of Eros as a Fisherboy* (43)
Perhaps based on a Hellenistic fountain group; features of Trajanic period.

15 *Portrait Bust of a Roman* (31)
Antonine.

16 *Bust of the Youthful Bacchus* (80)
Late 2nd century A.D.

17 *Bust of a Boy with a Bulla* (41)

18 *Portrait Bust of a Matron* (47)
Late 2nd century A.D. (Comparable to portraits termed Didia Clara, A.D. 193.)

19 *Bust of the Emperor Valerianus II or Saloninus, as a Young Child* (51)
c. A.D. 256–68.

20 *Head of the Emperor Marcus Aurelius as a Boy (A.D. 121–80)* (35)
Bust modern.

21 *Portrait Bust of a Roman Youth* (40)
Head, *c.* A.D. 215–30, on Trajanic bust.

22 *Head of a Warrior* (23)
(?) Later Hellenistic version of Pergamene group of Menelaos
rescuing the body of Patroclos.

23 *Portrait Head of Septimius Severus* (A.D. *146–211*) (36)

24 *Colossal Head of a Matron* (46)
Idealized portrait of a lady of the 2nd–3rd century A.D.,
resembling Julia Mammaea.

25 *Ganymede with an Eagle* (1)
Antonine (Restored).

26 *Celadon and Amelia* (105)
By John Charles Felix Rossi (1762–1839)

27 *Female Portrait Statue* (3)
Roman adaptation of 5th century B.C. original;
traditionally represents Agrippina the Younger as Ceres
(restored).

28 *Portrait Bust of a Matron* (65)
Late 2nd, early 3rd century A.D.

29 *Statue of Hera* (4)
Late Hellenistic, based on type of 5th century B.C.

30 *Head of a Girl* (48)
Roman copy of Greek head of the school of Praxiteles;
bust, Roman 3rd century A.D.

31 *Statue of Apollo Kitharoedos (The Egremont Apollo)* (5)
Antonine type, under 4th century B.C. influence.

32 *Head of the Emperor Antoninus Pius* (A.D. *86–161*) (77)
Renaissance bust.

33 *Head of the Emperor Hadrian* (A.D. *76–138*) (78)
Renaissance bust.

34 *Statue of a Satyr pouring Wine* (6)
Replica of an early work of Praxiteles; Greek inscription on support;
probably not contemporary
(restored).

35 *Head of an Athlete* (24)
Copy of bronze of 5th century B.C., possibly by Kresilas.

36 *Statue of Apollo* (7)
Copy of 4th century B.C. original of Praxitelean type.

37 *Head of a Youth in the Character of Hermes* (25)
Roman of Augustan age, style of Praxiteles.

The Carved Room

The Chapel

38 *Statue of a Satyr in Repose* (8)
Replica of a Praxitelean original; the head from another copy.

39 *Head of a Boy* (64)
Fragment (Julio-Claudian period) on modern bust.

40 *Dream of Horace* (111)
By Sir Richard Westmacott (1775–1856)

41 *Head of a Boy with a Fillet adorned with Ivy* (50)
Hadrianic period.

42 *Colossal Female Head* (27)
Perhaps part of a Roman temple statue fashioned out of the
fragments of two or more Greek statues. Face late Greek replica
of Artemis of Ariccia.

43 *Bust fashioned from a small Statue* (2)
Late Roman work.

44 *Statue of a Hora (Winter)* (16)
Roman work based on 4th century B.C. types.

45 *Gryphon* (82B)
Table leg (lower half restored).

46 *British Pugilist* (99)
By John Charles Felix Rossi (1762–1839)

47 *Nymph and Cupid* (98)
By Sir Richard Westmacott (1775–1856)

48 *St. Michael and Satan* (97)
By John Flaxman (1755–1826)

49 *Adonis and the Boar* (100)
By John Edward Carew (1785–1868)

50 *Apollo* (101)
By John Flaxman (1755–1826)

51 *Gryphon* (82A)
Table leg (lower half restored).

52 *A Nomarch of Dynasty XIX*
Egyptian black stone statue fragment.

53 *Statue of a 'Nymph of Artemis'* (17)
Graeco-Roman work based on 4th century B.C. type.
Inset in pedestal is:

54 *Slab of Pentelic Marble with Greek Inscription* (85)
Decree and list of names of 94 B.C. relating to Panathenaic
festival. (From Athens, perhaps from the Acropolis.)

55 *Arethusa* (103)
By John Edward Carew (1785–1868)

56 *Portrait of Lord Egremont's horse, 'Whalebone'* (89A)
Nineteenth-century bronze.

57 *Portrait Bust of a Boy consecrated to Isis* (49)
Roman 3rd century A.D.

58 *Head of a Boy, perhaps the young God Pan* (44)
Hellenistic type, possibly belonging to a fountain figure
(Bust does not belong).

59 *Statue of a Mourning Woman* (11)
Hellenistic type, 2nd or 3rd century B.C.

60 *Statue of an Amazon* (18)
Copy of a bronze statue of 5th century B.C. ('Mattei Amazon');
the head also a copy of an Amazon of the 5th century B.C.

61 *Seated Figure of a Philosopher* (19)
Head 4th century B.C. type, variant of Demosthenes (restored);
statue an Attic type of the Hellenistic period.

62 *Silenus Nursing Bacchus* (88)
Early 19th-century bronze copy from the antique.

63 *Seated Figure of a Man* (15)
Late Antonine copy of Hellenistic type, restored with head of
Emperor Gallienus (c. A.D. 218–268).
Inset in pedestal is:

64 *Greek Hero Relief* (72)
Late 5th century B.C. funerary stele in low relief.

65 *Torso Restored as Dionysos* (14)
Roman copy (reworked) of Polykleitan School.

66 *Statue of Pan and Daphnis* (12)
Roman. Late Greek head of Daphnis alien.
Inset in pedestal is:

67 *Greek Votive Relief* (13)
Fragment of Greek Votive Relief of the 5th century B.C. or a
scene of ancestor worship.

Paintings

The first number in each case is for identification purposes and is reconcilable with the number inscribed on the tablet beneath the frame

1 Thomas Phillips (1770–1845) (562)
*George O'Brien, 3rd Earl of Egremont (1751–1837) and
Mary, Lady Munster (d. 1842)*
She was Lord Egremont's second daughter.

2 W. F. Witherington (1785–1865) (27)
  Fête in Petworth Park (1835)

3 Thomas Phillips (1770–1845) (57)
  George O'Brien, 3rd Earl of Egremont (1751–1837)

4 Thomas Phillips (1770–1845) (309)
  George O'Brien, 3rd Earl of Egremont (1751–1837)

5 John Opie (1761–1807) (75)
  Card Players

6 Thomas Phillips (1770–1845) (59)
  William Wyndham, Baron Grenville (1759–1834)
  Statesman and nephew of the 2nd Lord Egremont. Successively
  Speaker, Home Secretary, Foreign Secretary, and head of the
  Ministry of 'All the Talents'.

7 James Northcote (1746–1831) (701)
  Hans Moritz, Count Brühl (1736–1809)
  Saxon Ambassador; amateur of letters and science; married
  the widow of the 2nd Lord Egremont.

8 Thomas Phillips (1770–1845) (504)
  Elizabeth, Countess of Egremont (1769–1822)
  Elizabeth Ayliffe married the 3rd Earl in 1801.

9 J. M. W. Turner (1775–1851) (656)
  Hulks on the Tamar (c. 1811)

10 William Hoare (1706–92) (538)
  Sir Charles Wyndham, 2nd Earl of Egremont (1710–63)
  Statesman; Secretary of State for Southern Department, 1761–63.

11 Sir Peter Francis Bourgeois (1756–1811) (6)
  Swimming Horses at Brighton

12 J. M. W. Turner (1775–1851) (91)
  Jessica—The Merchant of Venice, *Act ii, Scene V (1828)*

13 Thomas Phillips (1770–1845) (156)
  Hugh Percy, 2nd Duke of Northumberland (1742–1817)
  Great-grandson of the 6th Duke of Somerset.

14 Sir Joshua Reynolds (1723–92) (310)
  George Grenville (1712–70)
  Chancellor of the Exchequer; brother-in-law of the 2nd Lord
  Egremont.

15 J. M. W. Turner (1775–1851) (39)
  The Forest of Bere (1808)

16 William Blake (1757–1827) (427)
  Satan Calling up his Legions (Paradise Lost)

17 James Northcote (1746–1831) (92)
    Richard III and the Young Princes

18 Thomas Gainsborough (1727–88) (657)
    A Setter

19 Sir Joshua Reynolds (1723–92) (61)
    Macbeth and the Witches—Macbeth, *Act iv, Scene I*

20 Richard Wilson (1713/14–82) (360)
    View on the Dee near Eaton

21 Johann Zoffany (1734/35–1810) (659)
    An Actress

22 Richard Wilson (1713/14–82) (625)
    The Hermitage

23 James Northcote (1746–1831) (32)
    Princess Bridget Plantagenet dedicated to the Nunnery at Dartford

24 Richard Wilson (1713/14–82) (113)
    View on the Arno

25 Sir Joshua Reynolds (1723–92) (309)
    Death of Cardinal Beaufort—Henry VI, *Part II, Act iii, Scene III*

26 J. M. W. Turner (1775–1851) (21)
    The Thames near Windsor (c. *1807–8*)

27 William Owen (1769–1825) (13)
    Known as Mrs. Robinson

28 J. M. W. Turner (1775–1851) (46)
    Echo and Narcissus (*1806*)

29 William Hilton (1786–1839) (30)
    Rape of Europa

30 Sir Augustus Calcott (1779–1844) (22)
    Seapiece

31 James Northcote (1746–1831) (84)
    Lion Hunt

32 George Romney (1734–1802) (80)
    Mirth and Melancholy

33 John Hoppner (c. 1758–1810) (24)
    Sleeping Venus and Cupid

34 J. M. W. Turner (1775–1851) (33)
    The Egremont Seapiece: Indiamen and Man-of-War (*1802*)

44

35 William Blake (1757–1827) (454)
The Last Judgement

36 John Opie (1761–1807) (44)
Damon and Musidora

37 After Thomas Gainsborough (1727–88) (16)
Landscape: Children and Cattle

38 John Rising (1756–1815), after Sir Joshua Reynolds (304)
Charles James Fox (1749–1806)

39 Angelica Kauffmann (1741–1807) (60)
Diomed and Cressida

40 Thomas Gainsborough (1727–88) (106)
A Pool with Shepherd and Cattle

41 Studio of Sir Joshua Reynolds (1723–92) (162)
John Manners, Marquess of Granby (1721–70)
A distinguished soldier; he married a daughter of the 6th Duke
of Somerset.

42 John Hoppner (c. 1758–1810) (54)
Vertumnus and Pomona

43 Thomas Phillips (1770–1845) (268)
The Allied Sovereigns at Petworth, 24 June 1814
Lord Egremont is receiving in the Marble Hall the Prince
Regent, the Tsar Alexander I, the Grand Duchess of Olden-
burg, Frederick William III of Prussia and his son Frederick
William IV, and the Prince of Wurtemberg.

44 John Lucas (1807–74) (254)
Charlotte Wyndham, Mrs. King (1795–1870)
Third daughter of 3rd Earl of Egremont.

45 Thomas Phillips (1770–1845) (264)
William Scott, Lord Stowell (1745–1836)
Judge of High Court of Admiralty.

46 Thomas Patch (c. 1720–82) (357)
'*The Cognoscenti*'
The 2nd Earl of Egremont is with Sir Horace Mann, Capt.
Walcott, Mr. Apthorpe and an unidentified man.

47 Thomas Phillips (1770–1845) (695)
George O'Brien, 3rd Earl of Egremont (1751–1837)

48 William Blake (1757–1827) (408)
Characters from Spenser's Faerie Queene

49 John Lucas (1807–74) (253)
Frances Wyndham, Lady Burrell (1789–1848)
Eldest daughter of 3rd Earl of Egremont.

50 Thomas Phillips (1770–1845) (410)
Col. George Wyndham, 1st Baron Leconfield (1787–1869)

51 Sir David Wilkie (1785–1841) (87)
John Knox preaching before the Lords of the Congregation, 10 June 1559
A sketch for the picture in the Tate Gallery.

52 Washington Allston (1779–1843) (449)
Jacob's Dream

53 Philip James de Loutherbourg (1740–1812) (362)
Storm and Avalanche near the Scheideck

54 Henry Howard (1769–1847) (81)
Apotheosis of Princess Charlotte (1769–1817)
She was the only daughter of George IV and Caroline of Brunswick, and married Prince Leopold of Saxe-Coburg.

55 Henry Fuseli (1741–1825) (50)
The Wife of Bath's Tale—Chaucer's Canterbury Tales
On the reverse: *Group of five women.*

56 Sir William Beechey (1753–1839) (235)
Frances, Lady Burrell as Hebe (1789–1848)
Eldest daughter of 3rd Earl of Egremont.

57 Henry Fuseli (1741–1825) (402)
Macbeth and the Witches—Macbeth, Act i, Scene III

58 Sir Joshua Reynolds (1723–92) (105)
Charity

THE CHAPEL is the only major part of the Percys' medieval manor, apart from the cellars, to have survived intact. Lower in level than the Duke of Somerset's remodelled house it is also out of alignment with it, but compensation was made for this by the enormously thick wedge-shaped walls built either side. The window arcades are in the purest early English style with Purbeck marble columns set against local Sussex stone, and probably date from around 1309 when Henry, first Lord Percy, was given licence to crenellate at Petworth. The eagle lectern is a very fine late fourteenth-century example, and some of the window tracery may also be of this period.

Except for the lectern, the furnishings of the chapel date entirely from the years 1685 to 1692 and were commissioned by the 6th Duke of Somerset after his marriage to Lady Elizabeth Percy. The balustered communion rail was made by one Peter Voller in 1685 but almost all the rest is of 1689 and the two following years: the carpentry by William Burchett, the pulpit (more like a double reading desk) by Isaac Greene, the barrel-vaulted plasterwork ceiling by Edward Goudge, and the painting and gilding by George Turner. The accounts do not unfortunately mention carving, but John Selden was almost certainly responsible for this: the reredos carved with wheat and grapes symbolic of the sacraments is fairly conventional in design by City Church standards, but the marvellously expressive winged putti looking towards the altar from above each pew are equalled only by Gibbons's choir stalls in St. Paul's. The original graining of the woodwork and marbling of the urns above has also survived. The climax of this seventeenth-century decoration is the family pew, more like an opera box, at the west end, resting on a screen of Ionic columns and framed by a gigantic proscenium which is carved and painted to look like damask drapery. In the centre the Duke's arms and oversize coronet are borne aloft by angels. Perhaps nowhere in England is there so advanced an expression of the Baroque and indeed its prototypes are rather to be found at Versailles, or in Bernini's Cornaro Chapel at the church of Santa Maria della Vittoria in Rome.

The theme of wings, the Duke's crest, is continued by the two trumpeting angels painted on the side walls next to the family's pew. The artist of these and of the altarpiece with the Holy Spirit and a nimbus of cherubs is not known. The heraldic glass in the windows is mostly sixteenth and early seventeenth century depicting the arms of Percy ancestors, while those painted in the blocked up north windows are the 'Proud Duke's' additions, advertising his even more magnificent lineage with the arms of two kings, Henry VIII and Edward VI, in pride of place.

The Park and Pleasure Grounds

The contrast between the east side of the house, where the roofs of the town and church huddle up against the stables and offices, and the west side, looking far over the deer-park towards the lake, is one of the most exciting features of Petworth. But it was achieved more by accident than design. The enormous Elizabethan stables built by the 8th Earl of Northumberland stood until about 1725 on what is now the nearer shore of the lake directly opposite the Duke of Somerset's splendid new façade and dominating the view from it. Defoe described these stables as larger than many noblemen's houses, and criticized the Duke for not re-building afresh on the hill north-west of the old house, a site which would have avoided both this undignified prospect and the close proximity of the town.

The stables were indeed found to block the view too effectively and were pulled down in the Duke's lifetime, but the park was still very far from its present appearance. As was usual for a house of this date a formal garden with a symmetrical parterre and avenues was laid out. The parterre on the west front is known from a survey of 1751, but the accounts also speak of a black marble fountain, a Bowling Green and Greenhouse, a banqueting house in a wood, and 'flower potts upon peeres goeing up the ramparts'. These 'ramparts' were terraces cut into the side of the hill on the right looking from the west front. Also in the accounts are payments to the landscape-gardener George London and it is probable that he and his partner Henry Wise were responsible for the layout, between 1689 and about 1700.

Almost nothing remains of this baroque setting, for it was swept away in the mid-eighteenth century by Capability Brown. Brown's original design for the park at Petworth exists in the archives and is dated 1752, soon after the succession of the 2nd Earl of Egremont. Presumably in the next few years, while alterations were also being made inside the house, the landscape took on roughly its present form. The stream was dammed to make the lake, the park planted with clumps of trees, the Pleasure Grounds laid out to the north of the house and 'the Terrasses reduced to fine undulated steps Adorned with Groupes of Cedars, Pines, &c.' Brown's design also proposed a number of new buildings, notably a large 'Greenhouse' or Orangery just to the north-west of the house with a parterre in front of it facing south, a sham bridge at one end of the lake and a grotto the other, a summer house and a keeper's lodge with two octagonal towers on the hill above the lake. Some of these may have been executed, but have been demolished at a later date when a stricter feeling for Natural Landscape prevailed under the 3rd Earl.

The Pleasure Grounds which lie to the north of the house are however still very much as they appear on the survey of 1752, where they are called 'Cypress Walks'. Protected on the park side by a deep 'Foss to keep out the Deer', this roughly triangular plantation of oaks, evergreens and shrubs is laid out with walks and with two small buildings: on the northernmost edge a rotunda of ten Ionic columns (originally with a domed roof) which has wide views towards Midhurst, and a small Roman Doric temple nearer the house restored in 1949 as a memorial to Henry Wyndham, the elder brother of the late Lord Egremont who was killed at El Alamein. Both these buildings are shown in their present positions on Capability Brown's plan and could have been designed by him, though the Doric temple is labelled 'the situation for the Pavilion which now stands on the Terrass' and could therefore be an earlier building moved from the 'ramparts'.

Brown was still living at Stowe, completing the work which he had carried out there, when he was first approached by the 2nd Earl of Egremont in 1751. Accounts for that and the following year refer to his journeys to Petworth to inspect the house and grounds, and to preparing 'several plans for Petworth' of which the one already mentioned is a survivor. A contract between Lord Egremont and Lancelot Brown in the sum of £1,175 was drawn up on 1st May, 1753, and settled in 1754 in which year a further contract was made containing references to the 'plan for the lake in the park near the Half Moon Wood' (almost certainly that now called the Lower Pond). There are further contracts of 1st June, 1755 and 4th May, 1756, the latter mentioning the 'further new lake'. Meanwhile a considerable amount of material in the way of plants, shrubs and trees had been supplied by a nurseryman, John Williamson, to whom Brown refers in a letter of 1758, and one of whose earlier bills of 1753 gives an interesting list including 'spireas, Persian jasmins, Virginia sheemachs, tamarisks, bird and double cherries, American maples, sea buckthorns, trumpet flowers, roses, candleberry trees, broom, sweet briars, laburnums, lilacs and acacias'.

The 2nd Earl was one of thirteen peers who 'being well-wishers of Mr. Brown, whose abilities and merit we are fully acquainted with, do most earnestly request the Duke of Newcastle to promote his speedy appointment to the care of Kensington Gardens agreeable to his Grace's very obliging promises in that respect', an application which was not successful at the time, but which ultimately resulted in Brown being appointed Royal Gardener at Hampton Court, from where his letter of 27th October 1764 to the 3rd Earl (then only a minor) is addressed.

Brown's most characteristic contribution to the landscape at Petworth is of course the serpentine lake, enlarged from a small pond by judicious damming. The incomparable view this gave from the main front of the house was later to inspire some of Turner's most elegiac landscapes, with the deer silhouetted against the setting sun, and little has changed here since his day. Brown's clumps of trees on the ridges have now reached full maturity though the Duchess of Northumberland visiting Petworth in 1770 wrote that there were already 'Chestnuts, Oaks & Beeches of a stupendous size & surpass all that I have seen in my life'. She also recorded that 'the Parks are quite in Character, with the House Park quite decorated and smooth, [while] the Stag Park quite in the forest stile exhibits a pleasing Wilderness. The Stags add much to its Beauty by being in great number and remarkably tame'. The stag park was in fact cleared by the 3rd Earl about 1800 and turned into a model farm 'designed for experimental agriculture', but the herd of fallow deer still number over four hundred and graze in the 'house park' and around the lake often coming right up to the windows of the west front.

It was also the 3rd Earl who placed the superbly carved seventeenth-century urns on pedestals throughout the park and gardens including three on small islands in the lake, one on the ridge to the north-west of the house (the site of the 'ramparts'), and a particularly fine pair based on antique models flanking the north bay of his new sculpture gallery. Some of these may have come from the parapet of the west front, and others from the Duke of Somerset's formal parterre garden. The boathouse on the lake seems also to be of the 3rd Earl's time though the Neptune bas-relief between its two arches is again seventeenth century and possibly came from the 'fount house' erected in 1694. On a pedestal in the shallow waters of the lake directly opposite the centre of the house is a large stone hound, a memorial to one of the Earl's favourite hunting dogs which is said to have drowned there. Far away on the ridge above the lake to the north-west, and visible in winter from the house, is a Gothick folly with two turrets, pro-bably built about 1800.

Returning to the immediate surroundings of the house, the wrought-iron screens either side of the west front are replicas of Tijou designs and the gates into the park from the private gardens on the south are based on his gates at Hampton Court. The triton seated on three dolphins and blowing a conch in the centre of a circular pond near the south front must however be a survivor of the Duke of Somerset's formal garden, as are the superbly carved trophies on the piers of the main gate. Very French in inspira-tion these have in the past been attributed to V. Prost of Dijon who signs some drawings of them amongst the family papers. Prost was however a late nineteenth-century battle-painter and these drawings are far more likely to be studies from the sculptures rather than designs for them, especially as the trophies are shown in the early painting of the west front about 1700 flanking the entrance to the forecourt. When Capability Brown destroyed this fore-court and brought the park right up to the west front, the trophies were presumably moved to their present position on large eighteenth-century piers.

Set back from the drive between the gates and the house is the long façade of the stable block, with semicircular window frames flanked by pavilions and a central arch. Brown's proposals for the park in 1752 included large new stables to be built on the left of the vista from the west front to the lake. This idea seems to have been rejected in favour of a more open, natural landscape and the present stables were formed instead, about 1760, out of the existing complex of sixteenth- and seventeenth-century outbuildings. In the courtyard, which is now used as a visitors' car park, can be seen traces of Elizabethan walls and mullion windows fused with eighteenth- and nineteenth-century work. The charming symmetrical coach house with low-pitched roofs and pediment must, like the façade, be of around 1760. The stonework at its corners is specially rounded to avoid the rubbing of carriage wheels.

The lodge adjoining the gates, with a central pediment and carved swag on a white stone panel beneath, was probably built at the same time as the stable façade. It could have been designed by Matthew Brettingham, who built the 2nd Earl's London house in the 1750s and who is known to have helped him acquire paintings and sculpture for Petworth. The lodges on the Midhurst road are very similar and most of the fourteen-mile park wall was probably also built about 1755–60.

THE TENNIS COURT. Real Tennis has been played at Petworth House since the sixteenth century. The present court, one of the few remaining in the country attached to a private house, dates from 1872. The game is still played by the Petworth House Tennis Club and anyone interested should apply to the Secretary, Mr. Andrew Dawson of Farne House, Birdham, Sussex. *Access to the Tennis Court is for Club Members only.*

Short Bibliography

Edward Croft-Murray, *Decorative Painting in England 1537–1837*, vol. 1, London, 1962.

Rev. James Dallaway, *The Parochial Topography of the Western division of the County of Sussex*, vol. II, part 1, 1832.

Daniel Defoe, *Tour through the Whole Island of Great Britain, 1724–7.*

T. W. Horsfield, *The History, Antiquities and Topography of the County of Sussex*, vol. II, 1835.

Christopher Hussey, 'Petworth House', in *Country Life*, Nov. 28, Dec. 5, 12, 19, 1925; and articles on the collections of pictures and furniture in *Country Life*, Dec. 5, 12, 19, 1925 and Feb. 13, 1926.

James Lees-Milne, *English Country Houses: Baroque 1685–1715*, London 1971.

Hugh Wyndham, *A Family History—The Wyndhams of Somerset, Sussex and Wiltshire 1688–1837*, London, 1950.

Henry de Percy (1341–1408?) cr. 1st Earl of Northumberland (1377)

2nd to 8th Earls

Henry Percy (1564–1632) 9th Earl of Northumberland (Known as the 'Wizard Earl')

Algernon Percy (1602–68) 10th Earl of Northumberland

Joscelyn Percy (1644–70) 11th Earl of Northumberland

Lady Elizabeth Percy (1667–1722) m. (3) **Charles Seymour** (1662–1748) 6th Duke of Somerset (Known as the 'Proud Duke')

Catherine Seymour (d. 1731) m. Sir William Wyndham Bart. (1688–1740)

Charles Wyndham (1710–63) m. Alicia Maria Carpenter (1729–94) who m. (2) Count Brühl
2nd Earl of Egremont

George Wyndham (1751–1837) m. 1801 Elizabeth Ayliffe (d. 1822)
3rd Earl of Egremont

George Wyndham (1787–1869) cr. Baron Leconfield 1859

Henry Wyndham (1830–1901) 2nd Baron Leconfield

Charles Wyndham (1872–1952) 3rd Baron Leconfield

Hugh Wyndham (1877–1963) 4th Baron Leconfield

Edward Wyndham (1883–1967) 5th Baron Leconfield

Henry Wyndham (b. 1915) k. at Alamein 1942

John Wyndham (1920–1972) m. Pamela Wyndham-Quin
1st Baron Egremont & 6th Baron Leconfield

Max Wyndham (b. 1948) 2nd Baron Egremont & 7th Baron Leconfield

Carlyn (b. 1951)   Harry (b. 1957)

Algernon Seymour (1684–1750) 7th Duke of Somerset cr. 1749 (inter alia) Earl of Northumberland & Earl of Egremont

Elizabeth Seymour m. Sir Hugh Smithson (afterwards Percy) (1714–76) succeeded 1750 as Earl of Northumberland cr. 1st Duke 1766

2nd to 9th Dukes

10th and present Duke

The National Trust

for Places of Historic Interest or Natural Beauty

This booklet describes one of over a thousand properties preserved for you by the National Trust.

Founded in 1895, the Trust is today the greatest conservation society in Britain and the country's largest private landowner. But it is not a government department: the Trust is a charity with membership open to everyone. It relies on the voluntary support of the public and the subscriptions and gifts of its members to maintain beautiful country and buildings of architectural or historic importance for your enjoyment and that of future generations.

THE NATIONAL TRUST . . .

Owns houses of outstanding interest, many with superb paintings, furniture and porcelain; many fine gardens and some of the most splendid examples of English landscape design; woods and moorland, hills and lakes; some 2,000 farms; nature reserves including islands and fens; nearly 300 miles of unspoilt coastline; lengths of canal, wind- and water-mills, bridges and other industrial monuments; prehistoric and Roman antiquities; even whole villages;

Preserves them for your permanent enjoyment. The Trust is empowered, under Act of Parliament, to declare its land and buildings inalienable. These can never be sold, or even compulsorily acquired from the Trust without the express will of Parliament;

Encourages maximum free public access to all its open spaces (subject to the interests of farming, wild life and amenity) and opens more than 200 important houses, castles and gardens at a small charge which helps the Trust to maintain them in a fitting manner . . . Entry is free to National Trust members.

You can play a part in this great work of conservation by becoming a member of the National Trust. For details, please ask at your nearest Trust property for our leaflet 'About the National Trust' or write to the National Trust, Membership Dept., P.O. Box 30, Beckenham, Kent BR3 4TL.